Beyond The Ducts: Navigating HVAC Digital Marketing

Compiled by HVAC News Network

Introduction

In the ever-evolving digital landscape, the HVAC industry stands at a transformative juncture. While the core principles of heating, ventilation, and air conditioning remain rooted in tried-and-true practices, the avenues through which businesses connect with customers, talent, and innovations have shifted dramatically. The introduction of new digital platforms, combined with an increased societal dependency on online engagement, has redefined the HVAC industry's strategies for growth and visibility.

As of 2023, an astonishing 4.89 billion individuals worldwide are tethered to social media. This expansive audience, coupled with their increasing time spent on these platforms – averaging 151 minutes daily – underscores the boundless potential these channels offer for HVAC businesses. With the right strategy, HVAC companies have the opportunity to tap into vast communities, foster relationships, and position themselves as industry leaders in a space where consumers are spending a significant portion of their daily lives.

But the digital rabbit hole doesn't end with social media. The omnipresent Google clocks in an estimated 83.9 billion visits a year as of April 2023. This behemoth search engine, which began as a simple research project, has transformed into the world's primary digital directory, guiding billions to the information they seek. A staggering 40% of these searches are linked to local. This means that almost half of the users are seeking services, products, or businesses within their vicinity. For an HVAC company, this isn't just a statistic; it's a goldmine.

In 2022 alone, 98% of consumers turned to the internet as their primary tool to gather information about local businesses. This isn't a mere trend but a fundamental shift in consumer behavior. Gone are the days of relying solely on word-of-mouth or print directories. The modern consumer seeks immediacy, authenticity, and relevance in their search, and the internet delivers precisely that.

At HVAC Growth Engine, our mission revolves around creating more effective HVAC companies, Faster. Through the collaborative efforts of our teams and the core values that steer our direction, we understand the weight of these statistics. Our commitment is to empower HVAC businesses with the tools, insights, and strategies they need to thrive in this digital age. As we embark on this journey, one thing is evident: The HVAC industry, backed by the might of digital technology, is poised for exponential growth.

Welcome to the future of HVAC. Let's build it together.

Performing an In-depth Competitive Analysis

Why Competitive Analysis Matters

In the business realm, understanding your competitors is paramount. It's not about imitation or envy, but rather about gaining insights to refine your strategies, identify market gaps, and solidify your unique position. For HVAC businesses in the digital age, competitive analysis provides a roadmap for navigating the market terrain, identifying threats, capitalizing on opportunities, and carving out a distinctive niche.

Key Benefits:

Strategic Planning: It helps to anticipate market shifts and craft flexible strategies.

Informed Decision-making: Makes you aware of industry standards and best practices.

Risk Management: By understanding competitors' failures, you can avoid similar pitfalls.

Tools and Techniques for Competitive Analysis

There's no one-size-fits-all approach to competitive analysis; the depth and tools you employ will depend on your goals and resources. Here are some trusted tools and techniques:

SWOT Analysis (Strengths, Weaknesses, Opportunities, Threats): A holistic view of both your business and your competitors'. It helps identify areas for improvement and potential market gaps.

SEMrush or Ahrefs: These SEO tools allow you to analyze competitors' websites, uncovering keywords they're ranking for, backlink strategies, and more.

Social Media Analysis: Tools like Brandwatch or BuzzSumo can provide insights into competitors' social media strategies, top-performing content, and audience engagement.

Customer Reviews and Feedback: Platforms like Yelp, Google My Business, and industry-specific forums can provide unfiltered feedback about competitors.

Understanding and Identifying Your Top Competitors

Before diving deep, it's essential to know who you're competing against.

Competitors can be:

Direct Competitors: Those offering similar services in the same geographic area.

Indirect Competitors: Businesses offering similar services but in different areas or slightly different services that could replace yours.

Perceived Competitors: Companies that aren't necessarily in your industry but compete for the same budget of your potential customers.

By classifying competitors, you can better tailor your strategies and decide where to invest your resources.

Gleaning Actionable Insights from Competitor Data

Merely collecting data isn't enough; the magic lies in interpreting this data into actionable strategies.

Content Strategy: If a competitor's blog post or video is getting significant traction, consider creating better, more in-depth content on the same topic, ensuring you add your unique perspective or expertise.

Service Offerings: Are competitors offering services you aren't? Evaluate the demand and feasibility before diversifying your offerings.

Customer Engagement: If competitors have high engagement on social media or their website, analyze their strategies. It could be their response time, content quality, or engagement tactics.

Pricing Strategy: While you shouldn't imitate, understanding competitors' pricing can help in creating packages or promotional offers that provide more value.

Technology and Tools: Are competitors using a new tool or software that improves efficiency or enhances customer experience? Investigate its benefits and decide if it's a worthy investment for your business.

In conclusion, competitive analysis is not a one-time task but an ongoing process. The HVAC industry, like any other, is continually evolving, with new players, technologies, and customer preferences emerging. Regularly updating your competitive analysis ensures that your business remains agile, informed, and ready to seize new opportunities.

With the blueprint provided in this chapter, HVAC business owners can confidently embark on a journey of understanding their competitors, not as adversaries, but as invaluable sources of insights and learning. Remember, the aim is not to imitate but to innovate, taking the best from the industry and combining it with your unique value to create an unbeatable HVAC service.

Mastering Keyword Research for HVAC Businesses

The world of digital marketing revolves around the mighty keyword. These are the terms and phrases that potential clients input into search engines, hoping to find services just like yours. For HVAC businesses aiming to make their mark online, understanding keyword research is akin to discovering a treasure map. The right keywords can drive targeted traffic to your website, resulting in more bookings, inquiries, and revenue.

However, not all keywords are created equal. While some can bring a deluge of visitors, others might attract the right kind of visitor—ones ready to use your HVAC services. This chapter aims to guide you through the maze of keyword research, ensuring you identify those goldmine terms that boost your business.

Tools for Effective Keyword Research

Diving into the keyword ocean requires some nifty tools to help you navigate. These tools provide insights, suggest terms, and analyze the potential of each keyword.

Google Keyword Planner: A free tool by Google, it provides data on search volume, competition, and even ad expenditure for specific keywords.

Ubersuggest: Created by digital marketing guru Neil Patel, this tool gives keyword suggestions, search volume, and competitive data.

SEMrush: Beyond competitive analysis (as discussed in the previous chapter), SEMrush is a powerful tool for keyword research, offering detailed data on keyword difficulty, search volume, and more.

Ahrefs' Keywords Explorer: Similar to SEMrush, Ahrefs gives comprehensive insights into keywords, their potential, and how tough the competition might be.

Understanding Search Intent

Not every search is made equal. While some users might be looking for information "How does an HVAC system work?", others could be ready to make a purchase "Best HVAC company near me". Understanding this intent is crucial. Broadly, search intent can be categorized into:

- **Informational:** Seeking answers or more knowledge about a subject.

- **Navigational:** Looking for a specific website or page.

- **Transactional:** Ready to make a purchase or use a service.

- **Commercial:** Seeking out reviews or product comparisons before making a final transactional search.

For HVAC businesses, tapping into transactional and commercial intent keywords can be especially lucrative.

Finding Niche-specific HVAC Keywords

HVAC, like any industry, has its specific jargon and terms. These niche-specific keywords can be lucrative, as they often have lower competition and high specificity. Some strategies to uncover them include:

1. **Use Autocomplete:** Type in HVAC-related terms on search engines and see what autocomplete suggestions come up.

2. **Dive into Forums and Communities:** Websites like Reddit or Quora can be goldmines for niche terms and questions people have about HVAC.

3. **Think Like a Customer:** Consider the terms a layperson might use, rather than industry jargon. They might search for "noisy AC fix" rather than a more technical term.

Analyzing Keyword Difficulty and Search Volume

While finding keywords is part of the journey, understanding their potential is where the magic lies.

- **Keyword Difficulty:** Tools like SEMrush and Ahrefs provide a keyword difficulty score. The higher the score, the harder it will be to rank for that keyword due to competition.

- **Search Volume:** Represents how many times a keyword is searched for in a month. While high search volume sounds lucrative, if it's coupled with high difficulty, it might not be the best starting point.

Remember, sometimes targeting multiple lower-volume, lower-competition keywords can drive more traffic and conversions than targeting a single high-volume, high-competition term.

In summary, keyword research is both an art and a science. It requires understanding your audience, utilizing the right tools, and constantly refining your strategy as market dynamics change. For HVAC businesses, mastering keyword research can be the difference between a struggling online presence and a thriving, lead-generating digital platform. Stay curious, stay informed, and watch as the right keywords transform your HVAC business's digital trajectory.

HVAC Website Structure & Optimization

In the vast digital marketplace, your website serves as your HVAC business's virtual storefront. Its design, functionality, and accessibility can either attract potential customers or deter them. A well-structured website:

- Directs visitors effortlessly, ensuring they find what they seek.
- Epitomizes professionalism and trustworthiness.
- Boosts SEO since search engines favor user-centric sites.
- Enhances the conversion rate, turning site visitors into clients.

Mobile-first Design Considerations

The meteoric rise in smartphone usage mandates a shift towards mobile-first website designs. Such designs ensure that sites are primarily tailored for mobile displays, given the large user base accessing websites through these devices.

Key Elements of Mobile-first Design:

Responsive Design: It guarantees your website is adaptable, providing optimal viewing across various devices.

Touch-friendly Navigation: Think larger, tactile buttons and intuitive menus suitable for touchscreens.

Quick Load Times: Mobile users are usually on-the-move, so swift page loads are imperative.

Optimized Media Elements: Adjusting images and videos to suit mobile displays without sacrificing quality.

User Experience (UX) and its Significance

The user experience is the crux of your website. It encapsulates the overall feel and ease of navigation for your site visitors.

Why UX is Paramount for HVAC Websites:

First Impressions Matter: Your website's design and navigability are often the first things a visitor notices.

Retention: A seamless user experience ensures visitors remain on your site, exploring your offerings.

Conversions: An excellent UX design smoothly guides users through the decision-making process, culminating in service bookings or inquiries.

The Dominance of WordPress Websites for HVAC Businesses

In the evolving digital landscape, WordPress has emerged as a preferred platform for many businesses, including those in the HVAC industry. Here's why:

Flexibility & Scalability: WordPress is highly adaptable, suitable for small businesses and large enterprises alike.

SEO-friendly: WordPress websites are inherently structured for SEO, with numerous plugins available to further optimize your site.

Vast Ecosystem: A plethora of themes, plugins, and tools tailor-made for various industries, including HVAC, are available on WordPress.

Investing in a WordPress developer is a strategic move. While upfront costs are involved, the long-term benefits—like a professional-looking website and regular updates—outweigh the initial expenditure.

Optimizing Website Speed and Performance

A snappy website holds the power to retain potential customers. In the age of instant gratification, any delay can lead to lost opportunities.

Strategies to Boost Website Speed:

Image Compression: Utilize tools like TinyPNG to reduce image sizes without quality loss.
Utilize Browser Caching: Allow browsers to remember and swiftly load previously visited parts of your site.

Reduce HTTP Requests: Fewer scripts, images, and CSS files mean swifter site loading.

Streamline CSS and JavaScript: Minifying these files can lead to faster page loads.

The Role of Compliance (ADA, GDPR, etc.) and its Impact on Trust

Beyond the obvious legal implications, adherence to regulations like the ADA and GDPR fosters trust among your clientele.

ADA Compliance: An ADA-compliant website is universally accessible, even for those with disabilities—promoting inclusivity and avoiding legal pitfalls.

GDPR & Data Protection: With rising data privacy concerns, being GDPR-compliant underlines your commitment to data security.

Uncompliant websites risk being penalized by search engines and, more crucially, can face advertising bans, thereby impeding online marketing efforts.

To summarize, a well-optimized website for your HVAC business isn't just an online portal—it's a strategic asset. In an era where digital interactions often precede physical ones, your website's design, performance, and accessibility can significantly influence your business growth. Investing in platforms like WordPress and ensuring top-tier user experience can set your HVAC business on a trajectory for online success.

The importance of CRM systems and Follow Up

Customer Relationship Management (CRM) systems have become a foundational pillar in managing and understanding client interactions. At its core, a CRM system offers a centralized platform where businesses can track client communications, manage leads, document sales processes, and automate essential business tasks.

For HVAC businesses, this means an organized, comprehensive view of customer history, preferences, and feedback, positioning the company to better address customer needs and boost loyalty.

Importance of Follow Up

The HVAC industry is rife with competition. Ensuring consistent and meaningful engagement with your clients can differentiate your brand, fostering trust and ensuring customer retention.

Why Following Up is Crucial:

- **Building Trust:** Regular check-ins after servicing exhibit care and professionalism.

- **Gaining Feedback:** Post-service feedback can offer insights into areas of improvement.

- **Enhancing Loyalty:** Clients are more likely to return to businesses that show they value the relationship.

Automate Those Pesky Seasonal Reminders

For HVAC businesses, certain times of the year are ripe for particular services. Whether it's the pre-winter heater check or summer AC maintenance, seasonal reminders are vital. CRM systems can automate these notifications, ensuring timely alerts that prompt customers to book their essential services. This not only ensures steady business but also reaffirms your brand's commitment to proactive service.

Email Marketing Compliance Basics

In the digital era, email remains a potent communication tool. However, businesses need to be aware of certain regulations:

- **Opt-in Requirement:** Only send marketing emails to individuals who have explicitly agreed.

- **Unsubscribe Option**: Every email should have a clear option for recipients to opt-out or unsubscribe.

- **Clear Identification:** Emails should clearly identify your business and purpose.

Non-compliance can lead to hefty fines and damage to brand reputation.

SMS Compliance Basics - A2P 10 DLC

With the rise of mobile communication, SMS has emerged as a powerful marketing and communication channel. However, with this evolution comes new compliance requirements, especially in the US.

Understanding A2P 10DLC:

A2P 10DLC refers to a system allowing businesses to send Application-to-Person (A2P) messages via 10-digit long code (10DLC) phone numbers. Carriers in the US categorize all Twilio traffic as A2P, and this new A2P 10DLC system ensures better message deliverability and reduced filtering risk.

Steps for A2P 10DLC Compliance:

Determine Your Messaging Volume and Tax ID Status: This will dictate the registration process. For instance: Those with a Tax ID sending under 6,000 messages/day should register for Low Volume Standard Brands, Higher volume senders should register under Standard Brands, and Without a Tax ID, one should register a Sole Proprietor Brand.

Special Use Cases: For unique messaging types, be aware of additional requirements or carrier approvals.

Where To Register:

A2P 10DLC registration can be conducted in the Twilio Console. Businesses and ISV-type customers can also use the registration API for registration.

Remember, adhering to these regulations ensures that your messages reach your clients while maintaining trust and preventing potential legal complications.

In conclusion, CRM systems are more than just tools for organization; they're pivotal for nurturing relationships and ensuring your HVAC business stays compliant in a digital world. Following up through emails and SMS, while ensuring compliance, solidifies your reputation and ensures customers remember your dedication and professionalism.

Take the Next Step to Empower Your HVAC Business

Ready to simplify your customer interactions, automate essential tasks, and ensure compliance with a state-of-the-art CRM system? Don't navigate these waters alone.

Contact us at https://hvac.media and benefit from a robust CRM system, complete with 24/7 chat and Zoom support. Plus, our experts will walk you through SMS compliance. Equip your HVAC business for the digital age, and let's drive growth together!

SEO Basics for HVAC Professionals

In today's digital age, being visible online isn't just a luxury—it's a necessity. When someone's heater breaks down in winter, they're likely to Google a local HVAC specialist. If your business isn't on that first page, you're missing out. SEO ensures that your website appears for relevant searches, capturing potential customers when they need you most.

On-page SEO: Meta Tags, Headers, and Content Optimization

Meta Tags: These aren't just backend jargon. The title tag affects how your page is displayed in search results. The meta description can influence click-through rates.

Actionable Tip: Plugins like Yoast on WordPress give you the freedom the manage this information on different pages and posts seamlessly.

Headers: A well-structured page with clearly defined headers (H1, H2, H3) isn't just good for readers—it helps search engines understand your content hierarchy.

Actionable Tip: Review your site's main pages. Ensure each has one H1 (usually the page title) and use H2s and H3s for subheadings. Tools like Screaming Frog can help you audit your headings.

Content Optimization: The core of your site. Content should be high quality, relevant, and incorporate keywords without sounding forced.

Actionable Tip: Regularly update your content. Set a bi-monthly or quarterly schedule to review and refresh your website's key pages.

Off-page SEO: Backlinks and Local Citations

Backlinks: Think of these as votes of confidence. A backlink from a reputable site tells search engines that your content is valuable.

Actionable Tip: Joining your local chamber of commerce builds a backlink and gives you an opportunity with business owners who are likely homeowners, that also likely work with homeowners.

Local Citations: Being mentioned on other sites, especially local directories, boosts your local credibility.

Actionable Tip: Use tools like Yext to ensure your business is listed consistently across directories.

Technical SEO: Site Structure, XML Sitemaps, and Schema Markup

Site Structure: A clear, logical layout helps both users and search engines navigate your site.

Actionable Tip: Consider a site audit. Tools like SEMrush can provide insights into broken links or structural issues.

XML Sitemaps: A roadmap for search engines, helping them index your site.

Actionable Tip: Create an XML sitemap using tools like Yoast SEO (for WordPress) or Screaming Frog. Submit it via Google Search Console.

Schema Markup: This gives search engines more context about your content.

Actionable Tip: Use Google's Structured Data Markup Helper to start implementing schema on essential pages.

Google My Business

Google My Business (GMB): Your online business card. A complete GMB listing can boost local visibility. It is actually impossible to rank in the Google 3 pack without one. Just be prepared to submit business documents and/or videos of your facility to verify.

Actionable Tip: Claim and optimize your GMB listing. Regularly update it with posts, photos, and respond to reviews.

Optimizing Made Easier

SEO can seem daunting, but with the right approach and consistency, the results are worth it. If you'd rather have experts handle the heavy lifting, visit hvacbusinesswebsites.com for tailored solutions.

Online reputation management

The digital age has revolutionized how businesses interact with their customers, and the HVAC industry is no exception. Now, more than ever, a company's online reputation stands at the forefront of its success. Understanding and managing this intangible asset is paramount for sustained growth and fostering lasting client relationships.

Introduction to Public Relations and Managing Public Sentiment

Public Relations (PR) goes beyond mere marketing; it's about cultivating and preserving a company's image in the public eye. For HVAC businesses, this means presenting oneself as a trustworthy and reliable service provider in a market saturated with options. Begin by taking stock of your company's current online reputation. Look at every review, article mention, and social media comment related to your business. Understanding the existing public sentiment provides a foundation upon which improvement strategies can be built.

The Integral Role of Press Releases and Content Marketing

Press releases might seem old-fashioned, but they remain a robust tool in the PR arsenal. For an HVAC business, something as simple as launching a new eco-friendly service or initiating a community outreach project can be newsworthy. Establishing relationships with local media outlets can offer opportunities for positive exposure and position your business as a thought leader in the HVAC space.

Complementing press releases, content marketing offers a more long-term strategy. By publishing insightful articles, guides, or updates about the HVAC industry, businesses can demonstrate their expertise and commitment to customer education. Over time, this not only attracts potential clients but also nurtures existing ones by offering consistent value.

The Pivotal Nature of Online Reviews

In a world increasingly reliant on online research before making decisions, online reviews have become the new word-of-mouth. A slew of positive reviews can significantly bolster an HVAC business's credibility, whereas negative feedback can be detrimental if not addressed promptly and professionally. This underscores the importance of not just providing top-notch service but also encouraging satisfied customers to share their experiences online.

Navigating the Landscape of Review Management

Engaging with reviews is not a passive process. Every piece of feedback, be it praise or critique, offers a chance for the business to showcase its customer-centric approach. While words of appreciation can be acknowledged with gratitude, negative reviews present a unique opportunity. Addressing such reviews with grace, understanding, and a genuine commitment to resolution can often turn detractors into advocates.

Incorporating Reviews into Marketing Efforts

Once a solid base of reviews is established, it's time to amplify their reach. Whether it's by highlighting testimonials on a company website, incorporating them into email campaigns, or even creating engaging video success stories, positive feedback can serve as compelling marketing material.

In conclusion, while the realm of online reputation management might seem vast and complex, with a structured approach, HVAC businesses can harness its potential to the fullest. In doing so, they not only enhance their image but also cement their place as industry leaders in the digital age.

Harnessing Social Media for HVAC Businesses

In an increasingly digital world, businesses must evolve to stay relevant. The HVAC industry, traditionally rooted in hands-on service, is no exception. With consumers now relying heavily on online platforms to make informed decisions, social media has emerged as a pivotal tool in the HVAC professional's marketing toolkit. Mastering its nuances can significantly enhance brand visibility, customer engagement, and, ultimately, business growth.

The Rising Importance of Social Media in HVAC Marketing

The onset of the digital age has transformed the consumer landscape. Today, a vast majority of potential customers turn to social media not only for entertainment but also for recommendations, reviews, and to engage with brands directly. For HVAC businesses, this provides an unparalleled opportunity to reach a broader audience, showcase expertise, and build lasting customer relationships. No longer is it sufficient to simply have a functional website; an active social media presence has become a vital component of a comprehensive digital strategy.

Identifying the Right Platforms

While the temptation might be to establish a presence on every available platform, success lies in strategic selection. Each social media channel attracts a specific demographic and serves a unique purpose:

Facebook: With its vast user base, Facebook is ideal for reaching a broad audience. Features catering to business pages make it especially beneficial for sharing company news, promotions, and customer testimonials.

Instagram: Being a visually driven platform, Instagram excels at showcasing before-and-after photos of HVAC projects, behind-the-scenes looks at operations, and employee spotlights.

LinkedIn: This platform shines for B2B interactions. HVAC businesses can position themselves as industry thought leaders, share insights, and network with other professionals.

Twitter: A fast-paced platform, Twitter allows HVAC businesses to share timely updates, industry news, and engage in real-time conversations with both customers and peers. With its hashtag system, it's also an excellent platform for joining larger discussions and positioning oneself as a thought leader.

Pinterest: Often overlooked in the B2B sector, Pinterest has immense potential. Given its predominantly female user base, Pinterest offers a unique avenue to reach decision-makers in households. Many wives and mothers use Pinterest for home improvement and maintenance ideas. Sharing visually appealing infographics, maintenance tips, and HVAC decor aesthetics can be a strategic move to capture this demographic.

Crafting a strategy that aligns with the strengths of each platform ensures not only a wide reach but also targeted engagement with the right audience segments. By recognizing the diverse opportunities these platforms present, HVAC businesses can more effectively resonate with potential customers.

Crafting a Brand Voice and Strategy

Every interaction on social media is a reflection of the brand. Before diving into content creation, it's imperative to define a clear brand voice. Is the brand more formal and professional, or casual and relatable? This voice should remain consistent across all posts and interactions.

Moreover, a well-defined strategy lays the groundwork for social media success. This involves determining post frequencies, identifying key content pillars (e.g., educational posts, customer stories, company news), and setting clear objectives, be they brand awareness, lead generation, or customer engagement.

Engaging with the Community: Posts, Polls, and Stories

Active engagement is the heart of social media. It's not just about broadcasting messages but fostering two-way communication. Regular posts keep the audience updated, but polls can be used to gather feedback or understand customer preferences. Instagram and Facebook stories offer a more informal way to connect, be it through day-in-the-life snippets, quick updates, or Q&A sessions.

Joining and Engaging in Local Communities

Local Facebook groups have become bustling community hubs, often filled with residents seeking recommendations for services, including HVAC. Joining these groups and participating in discussions (without overt self-promotion) can position a business as a local go-to expert. By providing value in these communities, like answering HVAC-related queries or offering seasonal maintenance tips, businesses can organically grow their local clientele.

In conclusion, while the HVAC industry might seem worlds apart from the digital realm of social media, the two are becoming inextricably linked. By understanding and adeptly leveraging these platforms, HVAC businesses can not only elevate their marketing game but forge deeper, more meaningful connections with their customer base.

Crafting a Content Marketing Strategy

In the digital era, content has taken center stage as the primary means through which businesses communicate, engage, and build trust with their audience. For HVAC professionals, a well-thought-out content marketing strategy can be the difference between blending in and standing out.

Why Content is King

The adage "Content is King" isn't just a catchy phrase; it's a testament to the importance of quality content in today's market. When consumers face a problem, they turn to the internet for solutions. By providing reliable, informative, and accessible content, an HVAC business can position itself as an industry authority. Not only does this increase visibility, but it also fosters trust, turning casual visitors into loyal customers.

Long-Term vs. Short-Term Media: A Synergistic Approach

When crafting a content marketing strategy, it's crucial to understand the roles and benefits of both long-term and short-term media. Both have unique advantages and can be used in tandem to achieve robust and sustainable results.

Long-Term Media: As the name suggests, long-term media refers to content that has enduring value and presence. This primarily includes anything that can rank on Google, such as blog posts, landing pages, and videos embedded on your website. The main goal of long-term media is to provide evergreen content that can continuously attract and inform visitors. It's an investment, where the focus is on organic search traffic, which, while taking time to build, offers consistent and lasting returns.

Short-Term Media: Typically encapsulating social media platforms, short-term media is more transient. Posts on platforms like Facebook, Twitter, or Instagram have a shorter lifespan in terms of visibility. However, they offer immediate engagement, allowing businesses to connect with their audience in real-time. These platforms are perfect for time-sensitive promotions, updates, or sharing snippets and highlights from your long-term content to entice users to delve deeper.

Synergy Between Long-Term and Short-Term Media: While they serve different purposes, these media types should not function in silos. Instead, they should work together harmoniously. For instance, a well-researched blog post (long-term) can be broken down into bite-sized pieces and shared across social media platforms (short-term) over a span of days or weeks. Conversely, feedback and engagement from short-term media can provide insights into audience preferences, guiding the creation of future long-term content.

In essence, while long-term media establishes authority and drives sustained organic traffic, short-term media provides engagement and nurtures your audience. Together, they offer a balanced and comprehensive content marketing approach, ensuring HVAC businesses can connect with their audience at multiple touchpoints and throughout various stages of the customer journey.

Understanding Different Content Types

Blogs: These are versatile tools that can tackle everything from detailed explanations of HVAC concepts to company news. Well-researched, relevant, and regularly updated blogs can significantly boost SEO, driving organic traffic to your website.

Videos: As visual creatures, humans find videos engaging and easy to digest. A short video can explain intricate HVAC procedures, offer DIY maintenance tips, or give a virtual tour of your facilities. Platforms like YouTube also open up a new channel for audience engagement.

Podcasts: As the popularity of podcasts surges, they present an untapped market for HVAC professionals. Regular episodes discussing industry trends, interviewing experts, or even answering customer queries can help in building a dedicated listener base.

Infographics: For complex topics, infographics offer a visually appealing breakdown, making information easier to understand. They're highly shareable across platforms, amplifying your reach.

Planning a Content Calendar

Crafting great content is just half the battle. Consistency and relevance are key to maintaining audience engagement. By creating a content calendar, you not only ensure a regular posting schedule but also that the content aligns with customer needs and industry trends.

When planning, always have the end customer's needs in mind. For example, as winter approaches, a blog on "Preparing your HVAC system for winter" might be more relevant than a general maintenance guide. Aligning content with consumer pain points ensures it resonates and offers genuine value.

Another pro tip is to consider things that aren't directly related to AC or Heating but are directly affected by them. For instance, remote work is trending so home comfort is becoming more important so a list of things they could do to make it more comfortable or things to consider when you're expecting about preparing your home for a baby noting ideal temperatures.

Measuring Content Performance and ROI

Publishing content without tracking its performance is akin to sailing without a compass. It's essential to measure metrics like page views, bounce rate, engagement rate, and, most importantly, conversion rate. Tools like Google Analytics and the insights available inside different social media platforms provide comprehensive insights, helping businesses understand which content types and topics resonate most with their audience.

ROI isn't just about direct sales. Increased brand visibility, customer engagement, and trust are intangible benefits that a successful content strategy offers.

Experimentation within Brand Voice

While it's essential to maintain a consistent brand voice, it doesn't mean there's no room for experimentation. Once you have baseline data on what works, don't be afraid to innovate. Maybe your audience would appreciate a video series or an interactive quiz. While experimenting, ensure that the core messages remain consistent.

In summary, crafting a content marketing strategy isn't a one-size-fits-all approach. It demands a deep understanding of the HVAC industry, audience needs, and the dynamic digital landscape. But with meticulous planning, regular monitoring, and a touch of creativity, HVAC businesses can leverage content as a powerful tool in their marketing arsenal.

Innovating with Technology: QR Codes & NFC Cards

The technological landscape is ever-evolving, and businesses must stay updated to remain relevant and competitive. One such innovation that has gained traction in recent years is the integration of QR codes and NFC (Near Field Communication) cards in marketing. For HVAC businesses, these technologies can provide novel ways to connect with customers and offer streamlined interactions.

A Brief Introduction to QR Codes and NFC Technology

QR Codes (Quick Response Codes) are matrix barcodes readable by smartphones. When scanned, these codes direct the user to specific online content, be it a website, promotional offer, or any other digital asset. QR codes are versatile, cost-effective, and can be easily integrated into print and digital marketing materials.

NFC (Near Field Communication), on the other hand, is a communication method that enables two electronic devices, one of which is usually a smartphone, to communicate when in close proximity. NFC cards can be tapped against a smartphone to initiate a predefined action, like opening a link or activating an app.

Leveraging QR Codes in HVAC Marketing Materials

QR codes have found their way into various marketing materials, from business cards to service vans. For HVAC companies:

Product Information: QR codes can be printed on HVAC equipment. Customers can scan the code to access detailed information about the product, maintenance tips, or even tutorial videos.

Service Bookings: Place QR codes on flyers or brochures, leading customers to an online booking system, making the appointment process seamless.

Promotions: Special deals or offers can be advertised using QR codes. When scanned, the user might be directed to a coupon or a limited-time offer page.

Service receipts: When sending out invoices or receipts include a QR code with a reminder to provide feedback.

Using NFC Cards for Quick Customer Interactions

Business Cards: Instead of a traditional business card, HVAC professionals can simply tap clients' phones to lead them to the company website, a portfolio of services, or even initiate a call.

Feedback System: After servicing, ask the customer if they are willing to provide an honest Google review and then simply tap their phone. The easiest marketing strategy ever to train your team on. You can even create a competition out of it.

Best Practices and Potential Pitfalls to Avoid

While QR codes and NFC tech offer numerous benefits, it's essential to use them wisely:

Inclusivity: Ensure your NFC cards also have QR codes printed on them. This way, you won't alienate customers with older phones that might not support NFC.

Clarity: Always provide clear instructions alongside your QR or NFC prompt. Not everyone may be familiar with how they work.

Speed: The digital assets your QR or NFC method points to should be optimized for mobile and load quickly. A slow-loading page can deter potential interactions.

Security: Ensure the platforms or services you use for NFC or QR code generation are reputable to prevent any potential security breaches.

In conclusion, by embracing technologies like QR codes and NFC cards, HVAC businesses can innovate their marketing and service approaches, offering customers modern, fast, and interactive experiences. Proper implementation, coupled with a clear understanding of the tech, can lead to enhanced customer engagement and loyalty.

Bringing It All Together: Drafting Your Marketing Plan

In the digital age, especially for industries like HVAC that have historically relied on traditional methods of advertising and outreach, transitioning to a more organic digital marketing strategy can seem overwhelming. However, as consumer behavior has evolved, the advantages of digital outreach have become undeniable. To ensure you're reaching your target audience effectively and efficiently, it's essential to craft a solid organic marketing plan. Here's how you can begin:

Setting Clear Marketing Objectives

Before diving into the nuances of digital marketing, it's crucial to understand what you aim to achieve. Is your goal to increase brand awareness? Boost sales during the off-peak season? Or is it to position your HVAC company as an industry thought leader? By setting clear and measurable objectives, you provide a roadmap for your marketing endeavors and a benchmark against which you can measure success.

Actionable Tip: Define SMART objectives (Specific, Measurable, Achievable, Relevant, and Time-bound) to bring clarity and focus to your marketing goals.

Allocating Budget and Resources

Once your objectives are set, the next step is deciding how to allocate your budget and resources. H

ere's the crucial decision: do you build an in-house team or partner with a specialized agency?

In-house Team: Building an in-house team can offer more control over your marketing activities. However, it also means you'll need to invest in hiring, training, and retaining talent. Plus, the rapidly changing digital landscape requires constant upskilling.

Working with a Dedicated Agency: Partnering with an agency, especially one specializing in HVAC marketing, can provide you with instant access to expertise and experience. Such agencies are usually adept at anticipating industry trends, understanding the unique challenges HVAC businesses face, and crafting strategies accordingly.

Actionable Tip: Consider the long-term implications of your decision. While an in-house team might seem cost-effective initially, the continual need for training and the pace of digital evolution might make an industry-specific marketing firm more viable in the long run.

Continuous Monitoring, Testing, and Optimization

The digital realm offers an advantage traditional marketing often can't: real-time feedback. Tools and analytics platforms provide insights into how your campaigns are performing, who's engaging with your content, and which strategies resonate most with your target audience.

Actionable Tip: Embrace a culture of testing. A/B tests, where you change one element of a campaign to see which performs better, can offer valuable insights. Regularly review and optimize your campaigns based on these insights to ensure maximum ROI.

Staying Updated with HVAC Digital Marketing Trends

The digital marketing landscape is in a state of constant flux, with new trends and tools emerging regularly. For HVAC businesses, staying updated is not just about being aware of general digital marketing trends but also understanding how these trends intersect with the HVAC industry.

Actionable Tip: Dedicate time each month for research. Follow HVAC marketing blogs, join industry forums, or consider attending webinars and conferences. This will not only keep you updated but also provide networking opportunities and insights from peers.

Conclusion

Crafting an organic marketing plan is a meticulous process that requires clarity, strategic thinking, and adaptability. By setting clear objectives, wisely allocating resources, continuously monitoring and optimizing, and staying abreast of industry trends, HVAC businesses can ensure they not only reach but also resonate with their target audience in the digital age. Remember, the journey of digital marketing is ongoing; it's about iterative learning and adapting to ensure sustainable growth.

Conclusion and Forward Momentum

As we close this guide, it's important to remember that the digital landscape is ever-evolving. Success in the HVAC industry, like many other sectors, is not just about mastering the present but also about being prepared for the future.

Experiment, Learn, and Adapt: The digital marketing realm is not static. What works today may need tweaking tomorrow. Therefore, it's crucial to maintain a mindset of continuous learning. This involves experimentation, gathering data, understanding results, and iterating accordingly. Encourage innovation within your team, keeping an eye out for new tools, strategies, and platforms that could amplify your reach and resonance.

hvac.media: Your Dedicated Partner in HVAC Digital Marketing

In a digitally crowded space, standing out requires a combination of industry-specific knowledge, expert-led strategies, and a relentless pursuit of excellence. It's not about merely getting online visibility; it's about resonating with your target audience in a way that drives real results. And in the HVAC domain, this means not just understanding digital marketing, but deeply comprehending the unique nuances of the HVAC industry itself. This is where hvac.media, a division of HVAC Growth Engine, excels.

Dedicated Teams For Each Service

At HVAC Growth Engine, we believe in the power of specialization. Recognizing that each facet of digital marketing has its unique challenges and intricacies, we've built dedicated teams of experts for each of our offerings. This ensures that every campaign, every strategy, and every interaction is handled by professionals who live and breathe that specific domain.

Google Ads Mastery: Our Google Ads department is split into two specialized teams. Our PPC experts, armed with the latest strategies and insights, craft campaigns that resonate and convert. Complementing them is our team of 'Bloodhound' account auditors, who meticulously analyze every aspect of your campaigns, ensuring that every penny spent is optimized for maximum ROI.

Deep Dive with Social Media: Our dedicated social media team is always on the pulse of the latest trends, ensuring your HVAC brand not only has a voice but sings in harmony with the ever-evolving digital audience.

SEO Excellence: With a team solely focused on SEO, we ensure that your HVAC business is always at the forefront of search results, driving organic traffic and building a robust online presence.

The benefit of this approach? Precision, efficiency, and results that speak for themselves. By having experts in each field, we ensure that no detail is overlooked, no opportunity is missed, and every campaign is primed for success.

With HVAC Growth Engine, you're not just getting a service; you're partnering with dedicated specialists committed to propelling your business to new heights.

HVAC Specialization

In the vast realm of digital marketing, a one-size-fits-all approach simply doesn't cut it. At HVAC Growth Engine, we've honed our focus specifically on the HVAC industry, ensuring that every strategy, every campaign, and every interaction is tailored to resonate with the unique nuances of this sector.

Deep-Rooted HVAC Experience: One of our partners has been immersed in the HVAC industry since he was a child being a second generation HVAC technician. This deep-rooted experience provides us with invaluable insights, allowing us to understand the challenges, opportunities, and aspirations of HVAC businesses from an insider's perspective.

Google Ads Prowess: Our Google Ads team boasts an impressive track record in the HVAC space. With 11 years of dedicated experience, they've managed a combined total of 270+ accounts, handling an astounding $5.6 million in ad spend across the US, UK, and Australia. This extensive experience translates to campaigns that are not just effective but are laser-focused on the HVAC audience.

The benefit of our HVAC specialization? It's simple: unparalleled understanding and unmatched results. By immersing ourselves in the HVAC world, we ensure that our strategies are not just generic best practices but are true solutions crafted for the unique needs of HVAC businesses. With HVAC Growth Engine by your side, you're not just leveraging a marketing agency; you're partnering with dedicated HVAC specialists who are committed to driving your business to the pinnacle of industry success.

Apply To Work With Us

Digital marketing in the HVAC domain is more than just about clicks and impressions; it's about building trust, establishing authority, and driving growth. And in this journey, having a partner that understands not just digital dynamics but the intricacies of the HVAC world can be a game-changer.

HVAC Growth Engine, through hvac.media, offers you just that: a partnership that's rooted in industry-specific expertise and driven by a passion to see your business succeed. We invite you to leverage our deep-rooted experience and specialized teams.

Apply to work with us at hvac.media.

www.ingramcontent.com/pod-product-compliance
Lightning Source LLC
Chambersburg PA
CBHW050515290526
45786CB00007B/2569